debtcibel

AUDIO MUST PREACH

audiomustpreach.com

debtcibel

a non-technical sound book
that teaches the church
how to spend, when to spend
and who to spend it on

Darius Fong

DEBTCIBEL

Published by Audio Must Preach

Copyright © Audio Must Preach, 2012
All rights reserved.
ISBN-10: 0615635881
ISBN-13: 978-0615635880 (Audio Must Preach)

Printed in United States of America
Designed by Darius Fong

For Audra

CONTENTS

debtcibel

FOREWORD

The job of a church sound tech is often strenuous and usually thankless. Those who serve at this vital ministry post are the first to arrive and the last to leave, Sunday after Sunday. Great care is taken to juggle a thousand details before, during, and after each worship service or ministry event. A good sound tech willingly and faithfully sacrifices copious amounts of time and energy, enabling pastors and musicians to be heard, and sound their best, all the while striving to minimize distractions for those who have come to worship. Only a few will recognize the significance of a good sound tech and even fewer will take the opportunity to thank those who serve in this capacity.

And yet, good sound is something we've all subconsciously come to expect. We understand the value of good sound inasmuch as we don't like it when the sound isn't quite right. When the occasional technical problem occurs, and we're forced to think about the sound system, it's bothersome to us. Heads immediately whip 180° around revealing glares of disapproval aimed at the sound tech behind the console at the back of the room. By contrast, when the sound is excellent we are neutral and unimpressed

. We want the sound to be great, and we'd just rather not think about it. The average church sound tech is a volunteer audio enthusiast and very rarely a professional sound engineer. Nevertheless we desire, even expect, professional results.

But good sound isn't just something we expect, it's also something we need. Sound reinforcement and amplification are needed, more often than not, to communicate well at a church gathering. Astute church leaders will correctly assess that the right sound system and an excellent sound team are crucial, if elusive, components to an effective worship service. Even so, many churches languish in attempting to address their sound ministry needs and expectations. So, what is the solution? A completely new sound system perhaps? What is the first, second and third step to building an excellent church sound ministry? If you're asking questions like these, you've picked up the right book.

Darius Fong has done a great service to the church in writing *Debtcibel*. What you will find in the following pages is a practical and superbly helpful guidebook for how to make the right decisions when it comes to your church sound ministry. From building a sound team to purchasing new equipment, the principles found herein are applicable and invaluable, regardless of your church size or ministry context. It is with greatest joy that I commend this much-needed work to you, as I have worked in ministry with Darius for the better part of a decade, and seen these principles in action firsthand. The concepts and philosophies you will find in these pithy chapters have been developed, tested, and proven in the trenches of ministry. Further, Darius is a Grammy Award winning engineer whose brilliant creative and technical mind is out shined only by His love for the Savior and a desire to serve His church.

Because I have had the great privilege of benefiting from the faithful ministry and wisdom of Darius Fong, I am confident that this book will be of considerable profit to you as you endeavor to more effectively exalt Jesus Christ through the ministry He has given you. I pray you will be blessed by my dear brother's ministry as much as I have been!

John Martin
Director, Resolved Music

Your Partner In Ministry

People fall asleep in church. It is a fact. We have all seen the heads bobbing back and forth during a sermon. Perhaps even you have fallen asleep during a service. Different people have different excuses. They worked too late, the preacher is too dry, the sanctuary is too hot, whatever.

Have you ever suspected that the sound of a preacher's voice could also be the culprit? I am not referring to the natural tone but to the sonic quality of the preacher's voice when projected through the sound system.

Imagine yourself reading a book at home. The power in your area goes out, and you have no choice but to light a few candles. As you continue reading your book, your eyelids feel heavier and heavier. Before you know it you are fast asleep, your book is on the floor and your jaw open wide. A sermon that is poorly projected sonically can have the same effect as reading a book in dim lighting. Your brain is working overtime to make out what the preacher is saying and before you know it, you are struggling to stay awake.

The Importance of Sound

In today's churches, sound is the vehicle by which the gospel and truth are proclaimed. Sound amplifies preaching and music to millions of people every week. It is almost impossible for churches to operate without a proper sound system. Sound might not be the only reason people fall asleep in church, but sound is arguably one of the most crucial aspects of a church's ministry.

Excellent sound, however, achieves much more than keeping people awake. Sound is crucial in almost all areas of ministry. Sound finds its way into sanctuaries, patios, childcare rooms, recording devices, radio broadcasts and more. Sound teams interact not only with pastors and musicians but also with church members. They are involved with every part of the church service, setting up, tearing down, as well as the service itself.

I am not trying to put sound on a pedestal by giving it more attention than it deserves. I am simply demonstrating how sound holds together many parts of your ministry and plays an essential role in churches today.

An Epidemic of Overspending

As crucial as sound is, it is also widely misunderstood. Sound is like a cloud of mystery that hovers over churches. Through numerous conversations with church members, pastors and musicians, I have had the chance to clear up a lot of misconceptions they have about sound. Still, many of these misconceptions exist in churches today.

Many churches attempt to fix their sound problems by purchasing more equipment, when their problems are actually caused by poorly designed acoustics or a lack of operating skills and knowledge. Obscured by poor understanding of sound, churches are not able to focus on purchasing the right equipment that would fit their needs. Instead they buy gear that cannot be easily expanded upon as they grow in size, and they install brand new systems without taking into account the acoustics of their worship space.

Many churches wrongly think that digital mixing boards can solve all problems, so they rebuild entire systems around them only to find that they have invested a lot of money with no evident improvement.

Often times, churches do not understand basic principles of sound. They lack the vision to properly establish budgets to guide them through different phases of growth and expansion. They lack trained ears to help them maximize on equipment they already have and to focus on the real needs of the church. Consequently, their misconceptions have caused them to repeatedly overspend on sound.

To overcome overspending would require efforts beyond making fewer purchases. It is about strategically and purposefully allocating funds. But what is the difference?

Sound is expensive, and there is no way around it. From purchasing speakers, mixing consoles, and microphones to doing acoustic treatments and wiring, sound is one of the most expensive investments churches have to make. Every major step of growth is benchmarked with more spending. If the financial burden is further increased by misconceptions about sound and bad spending strategies, then overspending is not only due to the price of sound. Simply making spending reductions on sound will not solve the problem of overspending. To really get to the root, it will require a good understanding of how to spend, when to spend, and who to spend it on.

You may think 'epidemic' is too strong a word to describe this problem of overspending, but it alludes to the very widespread sound-related problems affecting churches today.

If you understand how far and wide this problem has really spread, to use the word epidemic would be no exaggeration at all. Millions of dollars have already been wasted, and churches do not even know where to begin when facing these investment decisions.

Overspending on sound is not a problem that can be solved one church at a time. To fight this epidemic, we must do it together. I wrote this book for the church, focusing not on the technical aspects of sound but on how to plan and budget for it with relentless dedication to godly stewardship, which is our calling.

Let's stop overspending.

Your Stewardship is Put to the Test

No matter how big or how small the amount is, the credibility of churches is at stake in the handling of our funds (John F. MacArthur, *Whose Money Is It Anyway?*). Many churches after spending close to one million dollars are taken by surprise when they realize that they have not acquired the system they needed, nor do they have people with enough skills to run it. I have witnessed budget cuts half way into a full sound system installation to save money, only to realize that fixing partially executed work at a later date comes at a price. And it is often expensive.

Measures can be taken to solve this epidemic. The sound ministry is where your church's true stewardship can be put to the test. How you allocate your budget and how you plan for phases of expansion reflect your ability as God's steward and your desire to pursue excellence.

Reversal of Priorities

In 2010, I was kindly asked to consult for a church in Florida. Upon my arrival, I was immediately brought into a meeting where the church administrators, the worship pastor, the musicians and the volunteers were all present. With no time wasted, they began to express their concerns and questions.

They had recently upgraded their system. They hired a sound contracting company for design and installation, but when it was finally finished, they found themselves dissatisfied with the results. They had already made a significant investment and could not afford to make any more mistakes. They contacted me, intending that I would help them make the right equipment purchases to solve their problems. They wanted to know what they should buy to fix their problems. Are you also asking these same questions?

Churches usually begin making sound-related investments with equipment purchases, which seems logical since investing almost always involves buying something. But it is safe to say that when it comes to church sound, purchasing more equipment in most cases does not provide the ultimate solution. In fact, buying more gear to fix problems almost always leads to overspending. The most common misconception is that good sound can be achieved simply by purchasing good equipment.

Churches might each have their own unique challenges, but they are all struggling with the same fundamental problem. Churches have completely reversed their priorities when investing in sound. Instead they must first take into consideration the acoustics of their worship spaces and the realistic skill level of their teams. Investing in sound should not begin with equipment purchases.

Starting with Good Sound

Good sound begins with good acoustics. To understand this, you need to first understand that sound is a physical property that cannot be seen, but it is very real. It can generate enough force to shatter objects like glass or be used as a weapon to destroy. Sound is limited by other physical objects, and it is controlled by the space it lives within.

A space can be a sonic black hole, causing sound to project poorly regardless of what you do or what equipment you use, and a different space could act like a concert hall, accentuating and beautifying every audible frequency.

Acoustics should take first priority in shaping your thinking about sound. Even if you are not currently in the position to correct your acoustics, understanding your limits with poor acoustics will help guide your thinking when making future sound investments.

Your Gear is as Good as the Operator

Having observed many world-class sound engineers, I can tell you that great sounding records do not always come from the best equipment. Of course, great equipment can contribute to sonic quality, but only when it is operated by the right people. I have heard the best sound engineers make magic with mediocre equipment. Trust me. It is possible.

When I was ten, I wanted to be a painter. My mother, as encouraging as she always was, went to the art store and bought me the best supplies she could find. I had all the brushes, paints and colors I could ever want. I was excited to prove myself as a painter. I sat next to the window and painted everyday. A month went by, and not only did I not see any improvements, I could not even make out what I was painting from looking at my own work.

Sadly, all the best and plentiful supplies did not make me a painter, but it helped me realize what I was not. It is similar in the world of sound. Just as the supplies are only as good as the painter who uses them, sound gear is only as good as the operator. Purchasing great gear without a team of skilled sound operators to run it would still produce sound that is mediocre.

The church in Florida intended for me to help them make equipment purchases that would improve their sound quality, but after my initial interaction with them, I quickly realized that nobody there had ever been trained to run sound. Volunteers were ready and eager to serve, but nobody had the real world knowledge or experience to operate the equipment. Instead of helping them with purchase orders, I decided to focus on training. Within a couple months, they were giving each other listening assignments and critiquing each other's mixes. Some even enrolled in online audio courses. They were helping each other grow in their ability to listen more critically. I could not have been more thrilled.

This church was already growing in size and would eventually move into a bigger building. Allocating funds towards retrofitting the current building would have only been a waste. Focusing on training not only improved the sound quality in their current worship space, it also better prepared them for when they finally transition to the next building.

The Three Musketeers of Sound

Without the skills and proper understanding to use the equipment, investing in sound gear will only yield diminishing returns. Prioritizing investments does not mean neglecting one thing for another. All churches need equipment in order to run their services. Do not confuse adjusting your priority of thinking with holding out on purchases until the last possible moment. The important thing is to know what, why and when to buy. When assessing equipment that you already have or something that you are considering buying, you must understand the limitations and inter-dependability of acoustics, skill level and lastly, equipment. They are, as I call them, the three musketeers of sound.

Great audio gear is capable of delivering superb sonic quality as well as additional features that will grant operators more flexibility. But with more flexibility also comes greater responsibility. The added features often mean more work for the operator. There are more channels to monitor, more sources to connect and more components to control.

You need trained men to operate your gear and make the most of your investments. Your purchase cannot be maximized until your sound team understands how they are benefiting from it. They have to be able to hear the difference.

Making Sound Invisible

Sound is undoubtedly one of the most crucial aspects of your ministry, but it should not be the focus of your worship service. Sound should be invisible. It should never draw attention to itself or be a distraction during your service. It should enhance your message without being noticed. Sound becomes a distraction when it is poorly projected or overly amplified, because people are struggling to hear.

Sound is also a distraction when churches mishandle thousands of dollars on the wrong sound system, when they should be setting examples of good stewardship. For sound to be truly invisible and serving the Body of Christ, churches must strive to establish a clear vision to which they can be held accountable.

This is a big picture moment. You need to take a big step back to discern all your needs. Examine previous measures that have already been taken, and go back to the drawing board to establish a vision that will guide your church through future phases of growth and expansion.

There is not a standard that blanketly applies to all churches when it comes to sound. People attend church each with their own set of expectations, and experienced or not, they are extremely opinionated when it comes to sound in churches. In order for you to guide your church through important sound decisions and stop overspending, you need less technical knowledge of sound and more pastoral discernment.

To engage sound as your partner in ministry, you must employ creativity when making budget decisions and be able to foresee future phases of expansion. You need to get rid of any common misconceptions, observe your church from every angle and focus on the right strategies. You must be able to use discernment, which only comes from God.

You are not alone in this, as many churches are struggling with the same problems of overspending. Sound should not be a barrier for your church. It should be your partner in ministry to bring the gospel to people with clarity and strength.

Sound is Misunderstood

Imagine a magical knob that controls your church's sound volume like the master knob on your home stereo. You have probably wished for this knob at some point for your church. But, alas, sound cannot be turned down with an imaginary master volume knob. It just does not exist.

If you are at home listening to music, you can turn it up as high or down as low as you want. But even at home, there is a point when the music is too low to be audible or the noise of the air conditioner is drowning out the music for instance. The point at which the music is no longer audible to you varies depending on how much background noise there is. If there were a lawn mower mowing away next door, that threshold would rise drastically.

The biggest difference between sound at your home, also referred to as controlled sound, and sound at your church can be summarized by the term *Sound Reinforcement*, which is a fancy way of saying that projected sound functions to reinforce sound that already exists.

Without any amplification, there will still be organic sounds coming from the choir, piano, guitar amplifiers or drums. Unless your worship space is so large that there is almost absolute isolation from the stage to the congregation, sound reinforcement at your church will always be a blend of natural and amplified sounds.

The Universal Concern: It's Too Loud!

In the context of church, there is one universal complaint that always seems to ring in a pastor's ears. "The sound level is too loud!" Pastors, being sensitive to church members, have evolved into sound level sheriffs, setting sound level ceilings for their sound operators to abide by. Most people describe sound by describing how loud it is. You often hear people say," It sounded pretty good, because it wasn't too loud."

Turning down the volume at your church is not as simple as turning down your stereo system at home. There is a bottom threshold for each room that mix levels cannot go below. This threshold differs from room to room as determined by the acoustical properties, size, number of people and sound level on stage. If a sound operator turns down the mix level enough to be noticed, the apparent level is lowered, but chances are the overall sonics will start to suffer. Materials pushed through the speakers will become unintelligible. This is commonly described as muddy.

Personally, I do not know of any church sound operators who intentionally mix loud. On the contrary, most of them are more concerned about how loud they are mixing than you are. If your operator is not lowering the sound level to your desire, he is probably not able to lower it and still deliver a clear mix.

How then would he go about turning it down? If it really is too loud in your worship space, you would need to take measures to reduce the sound level. Good sound begins with good acoustics. Reducing sound level will also have to begin with acoustical treatment. Before investing in another piece of equipment, consider whether the acoustics of your worship space is contributing to the loudness and what it would take to correct the issue.

Absolutely magnificent old churches exist all over the world that were built hundreds of years ago. What is often overlooked when people admire these buildings are the contributions of acousticians who worked hand in hand with architects to craft these buildings. These buildings served to amplify sound naturally without additional amplifications. People even use the word *church* to describe large and reverberated spaces. Record producers, when referring to larger spatial treatment for a particular sound, often request for a 'church' sound. Most churches today no longer sound large and reverberated. They have expanded their musical styles past chanting and playing string instruments. Though some churches still hold to the traditions of organ and choral worship, many have adopted more contemporary music styles. An acoustic space that amplifies and reverberates like an old cathedral would be overbearingly loud for contemporary worship.

Your church might not be a cathedral, but like many old church buildings, it was not acoustically treated to suit music styles of churches today. Having a worship space built or treated to specifications acoustically is the only way to control sound levels.

Prioritize your spending wisely, and make acoustics your first priority. If you are planning for a building expansion, be sure to work with the best acoustician you can find. If you don't have a church building yet, or if your budget does not allow, work it into your future plans and budget for it. It is totally understandable that you may not be able to do much about your acoustics right now. Planning and budgeting for acoustics also takes time. If you are wondering whether there are any measures that can be taken to reduce the sound level. Good news. There are.

Turn Down the Noise

The first thing you can address is turning down the stage noise.

Halfway through a pleasant record that you were enjoying, your 10-year old son conveniently decides to bang on his newly acquired drum kit downstairs. You have no choice but to turn your music up to drown out the drum sounds. You find this is the only way to differentiate between the music you were listening to and the drum noise coming from downstairs.

Our ears do not discriminate. They take in everything. And we are incapable of turning off one sound to focus on another. When there is a lot of sound coming from the stage, the only way for the sound operator to help the congregation differentiate between sound projected towards them and sound projected for the musicians on stage is to turn it up, the same way you turn up your music when your son starts banging on those drums.

The louder the stage, the louder the projected sound towards your congregation needs to be. It also works the other way around. The louder the projected sound, the louder the stage needs to be. It is a vicious cycle.

Start by working together with your musicians and arranging them in such a way that they can hear each other without having to over amplify themselves. Have them play according to the size of the room. This not only helps overcome stage sound level problems, it also helps the overall sonics.

Shoot the Sheriff

I empathize with you if you find yourself acting as the sound level sheriff with a meter in your hands, but those numbers are not as meaningful or helpful as you might think. Acting as the sound level sheriff for your church can be very frustrating. You are already bombarded by many different matters of the church. There is no need to monitor the sound level for your services too.

Mothers are worried that it is too loud for their babies. Others are worried that their own hearing might be damaged. I understand your concerns for your congregation, but not all of these concerns are legitimate and monitoring your sound levels will not likely solve the real problems you have. Being able to differentiate legitimate concerns will prove to be very helpful as you strive to better serve your congregation.

If you have ever been to a live rock concert, you know that your sound level at church is nothing in comparison. If you thought it was too loud at the concert, you were probably right. Rock concerts are infamous for being way too loud.

My ears cannot usually withstand a full concert without earplugs.

A very common misconception about hearing loss is that loud spikes of sound are responsible for the damage. The truth is that most hearing loss is not caused by extremely loud spikes of sound but by exposure to loud sounds over long periods of time. A person would have to be exposed to loud sound levels consistently over an extended period of time to really be affected.

Dave Wilcox, who is the technical director of Covenant Life Church, conducted an experiment at his church using a formula derived by the National Institute of Occupational Safety and Health (NIOSH) that was put together to determine the safety of volume levels. He measured the sound levels of their services running between 85-95db and plugged these numbers into the formula. What he discovered was that even those musicians who are in the auditorium all morning long are far from experiencing any hearing loss.

Human beings have a daily quota of sound that we can be exposed to. The louder the sound is, the faster we reach that quota. Being at a loud concert, your quota will likely be met within half an hour. The volume levels at these concerts are at least three to four times louder than the average church service.

Most services last for about one hour with the music portion lasting for about half an hour. Unless you place your speakers right against someone's ear, I doubt there would be enough sonic power to damage a person's hearing with a one hour long worship service.

When dealing with mothers with babies, you can assure them that only babies with super-human hearing are in danger of experiencing damage. People often think that babies are more prone to hearing loss because they have more sensitive hearing, but that is simply not true. Babies are capable of hearing a slightly wider frequency range than adults due to the fact that their ears are brand new, but they ultimately have the same hearing mechanism as adults. They are not more prone to hearing loss.

Our Ears Are Uniquely Created

Consider this. When an awestruck documentary narrator on National Geographic informs us of our inferior hearing compared to animals like cats and dogs, what they fail to mention is that cats and dogs are actually incapable of hearing and understanding music and speech the way human beings can. Human ears might not be able to pick up frequencies beyond our created limits, but our ears along with our brains are created superior to the animal kingdom in the context of music and speech. We hear music and speech when they hear only noise and sounds.

The reason why sound meters alone are not useful in judging loudness is because our human ears are not created to listen like a sound meter. Human ears respond to different frequencies of the same level in different ways. We are much more prone to hearing mid range frequencies (1-4kHz) than we are to hearing lower frequencies.

For instance, a scale measures how much we weigh, but it cannot tell us whether we are healthy or not. If we gain weight, a scale does not tell us whether we have gained muscle or fat. A scale is a helpful aid to inform us only about one piece of information regarding the complete picture of our health, but it cannot be used alone to determine our general level of health. Other factors must be taken into consideration.

With regards to sound, these other factors are related to frequencies and how they behave under various circumstances. We should trust our ears to be an instrument of reference and to interpret data gathered from sound level meters appropriately alongside with a frequency scale.

A projected music program sitting at a comfortable volume with a sharp, bright vocal can give the congregation the illusion that everything is too loud. A loud program of a ballad, on the other hand, with tamed dynamics could appear to be warm and emotional instead of overbearing. Balance of frequency spectrum contributes heavily to the apparent level of sound. The apparent level is the level perceived by the listener, telling the brain whether it is loud or soft.

If you have been adamant about what the meter reads, I encourage you to put down the meter and start trusting your ears. You might not be a sound operator, but you probably have better hearing than you give yourself credit for.

Drum Shields Are Megaphones

Surprisingly, drum shields are another contributing factor to loud sound in churches. One might think they are using drum shields to reduce the drum noise level, but the way they are often used in churches inadvertently makes them act like megaphones that amplify sound.

Let's be clear. I am not implying that plexiglass, which is what drum shields are made of, amplifies sound. Drum shields are not made to amplify, they are made to reflect. They can be useful to prevent drum sounds from aiming directly towards a congregation. However, a drum shield is not meant to be used by itself without sound absorption treatment. Remember that sound is a physical property even though it is invisible. When it is reflected with no absorption, it will rebound to multiple destinations until the energy from the sound is exhausted. Many churches place their drummers in a corner with drum shields inserted between them and the congregation. Corners act as a focal point that projects and amplifies sound sources. Picture the shape of a megaphone or a person who is standing far away with both hands cupped around their lips, crying out to someone. Corners have the same effect on sound, which is to amplify.

When sound energy bounces back toward a corner, the corner will serve as a megaphone.

Churches employ drum shields to help reduce the impact of drums. Even when the drum kit is not placed in a corner, drum shields are seldom helpful unless the drummer is completely enclosed inside the shield with foam-like absorption materials. When drum shields are not setup properly, cymbal crashes and hi hats will still leak sound everywhere.

A better solution would be to configure the drums more appropriately for the size of your worship space. An electric drum kit can be an option, but it is not the only option. Drummers can choose to be very creative with their drum kits. They can use smaller sized drums or cymbals, or they can also use sticks that are not as loud. Collaborate with your music team and sound team, and find the appropriate solution for your church.

Fixing Feedback

Feedback is another problem that many churches face. Feedback happens often in churches. People have come to expect it, but that does not make it any less annoying. When it occurs, people react in panic and cover their ears. There is probably not another aspect of sound that people despise more than loud feedback. Feedback is the word that sound operators do not want to talk about.

So what is feedback? Feedback is an audio signal feeding back into its original source. Most of you were instructed at some point in your life not to point a microphone directly towards a speaker. To be more precise, you are not to point a microphone towards a speaker that is also feeding you its own signal. Most stage microphones are extremely directional. The back is designed to reject sound and the front is designed to receive sound. Properly placing your microphones will help eliminate feedback. You can also reduce the chance of feedback by speaking directly and closely into a microphone. Feedback is often caused by over amplifying an audio signal. By speaking directly into the microphone, you avoid the need for the operator to turn you up, which is when feedback occurs.

Feedback can also be significantly controlled by acoustically treating your room as well as tuning your main speakers properly. This part of design is too often overlooked in church building and remodeling plans. Treating your room will create a more even distribution of frequencies and tuning your speakers can eliminate exaggerated frequencies in your worship space, which will allow for optimum operating level of your speakers. It takes preparation and care, but feedback can be eliminated.

The Great Digital Divide

A very common misconception that I encounter is that digital mixing boards can solve all the world's problems, at least when it comes to sound. Maybe it is because of the flashy lights or the faders that can flip through pages. Or maybe it is the nice touch sensitive flatscreen that can be used to control the signal. I often hear people say, "It just sounds better with a digital board."

I have been asked numerous times to help purchase digital mixing boards, but personally, though I think digital mixing boards can make great tools, many times churches are acquiring them for the wrong reasons. They believe that buying a digital mixing board will significantly improve the sound in their worship space. In reality, digital consoles do not deliver superior sonic quality to an analog mixing board. They are simply designed with more emphasis on convenience.

Digital consoles are like digital snapshots of an analog console's interface. Electronically speaking, digital consoles are almost exactly the same as an analog console, except that signals are converted to digital and back to analog. In some cases when converting signals to digital, sonic quality will actually end up suffering in exchange for convenience.

Having a physical collection of books is very much like having an analog console. At one glance, you can see all your books organized in the way you prefer. On the contrary, a digital library on your computer with services like Amazon or Apple iBooks is very similar to a digital console. All your books are packed in one small device, making it convenient to carry. The down side to one of those devices is that you would not be able to see all your books at a glance without scrolling through. This is very similar to a digital console in that operators are not able to view all their settings at one glance without scrolling the faders.

The obvious advantage of a digital console over an analog console is space. A digital console integrates multiple tools like equalization and compression into a computer. Since all the tools that are traditionally stored in big equipment racks are now inside a computer, an operator with a digital console would require a lot less space than an operator with an analog console.

Another advantage of digital consoles is the ability to save and recall settings when a church has a very big setup. If your library spanned rooms or even buildings, you would probably need a computer to help keep track of all your books. A digital console offers similar conveniences, but keep in mind that these advantages have nothing to do with sonics directly.

Better tools only benefit operators with complementing skills. Without a trained team, chances are that introducing a digital console will only invite disaster. Since digital consoles are modeled after analog consoles, starting off with analog consoles could aid in training better operators. The decision between a digital board and an analog board really lies with the skill level of the operator. The skill level of your operators should always be taken into consideration. After all, a mixing console is just a tool.

Focus On The Right Things

Getting to the Root

Sound is extremely subjective, especially when you combine it with music. The difference between loud and soft for many people is often just a change in music genres with no regard to the actual volume. Mixing boards become designated help desks. At the sound board people voice their opinions freely as well as their complaints.

Dealing with concerns and questions from your congregation should not be new to you. As the leader of your church, you often have to deal with complaints. The challenge lies in your ability to discern. When a member of your church voices his opinion about a sermon, you have to differentiate between a genuine desire to understand scripture and a hardened heart towards the Word. It is no different when people complain about sound.

When your friend describes a new album to you by saying that it sounds amazing, he is not describing how well the drums are recorded or how well the microphones are positioned, he is merely expressing how the music makes him feel.

People often confuse music for sound. Complaints about sound in churches are not always about sound. When dealing with concerns or complaints, getting to the root of the problem might not be easy, but it will be instrumental in preventing overspending.

Focusing on the right things means establishing a strong partnership with your sound team. You need someone to help you, someone with the ability to assist you in making the right investment decisions. You need sound mixers who are not merely equipment operators, but mixers who love to serve their church. This is an important step towards maximizing your existing investment and developing a strategy for future investments that is centered around the real needs of your church.

Mixers Who Love the Church

I have been to churches where sound operators simply functioned as technicians who controlled the on and off switch of the sound system. They have the technical knowledge to turn a few knobs and push a few buttons but not the desire to improve and learn. They ignored the needs around them and put up barriers, making it difficult for everyone, including pastors, musicians and church members to interact with them. Their negative attitudes dragged down everybody around them.

There are many technical requirements for a sound operator, but even more important than technical requirements is a love for the church and a genuine desire to serve. I was extremely encouraged by the church in Florida and their sound team. Everybody was eager to serve and learn. They loved their church and were excited to learn. They were humble enough to help each other grow by critiquing each other's mixes.

If a mixer lacks knowledge but has all the right qualities and the right attitude, then all that is necessary is training and time. On the contrary, if a genuine desire to serve is lacking, no amount of training will make him care. Training will not produce a servant. It is always better to find someone who cares.

The right mixer will function not only to operate the sound board weekly but play an important role in helping make sound investment decisions that will serve the church. You need more than an operator, you need a mixer who cares and loves the church.

A sound mixer is the leader of a sound team. He is responsible for making decisions that will affect the quality of sound, but it is just as important for him to lead spiritually as it is to lead technically. He is to encourage and remind his team to serve and set an example through his leadership. A mixer who is a true leader understands the needs of his church and serves his church, not his own agendas. He is a true servant at heart.

Most people do not realize this, but sound teams often have the last interactions with pastors and worship leaders before they step on stage to lead the congregation to the throne of God for worship. They have unique opportunities to serve their pastors and others who are also serving every week.

Their attitude towards others can either serve to encourage or distract. Therefore operators who are skilled but incapable of leading and serving others should be disqualified as mixers.

Sound mixers also need to be able to listen critically. Not everyone who has a servant's heart can be qualified to be a mixer for his church. The same way a gifted pianist communicates immense amount of emotion through the piano, a gifted mixer with musical ears can conduct music beautifully through the console.

Everyone including those who do not have superb hearing can volunteer to be a part of the sound team to assist with setups and tear-downs, but not every person is capable of being in charge of sonics. We are not created equally, and we all play different roles in serving the church body. A mixer needs to possess the unique ability to listen critically and accurately.

No amount of investment can hide untrained ears behind the mixing board. Even if you are not in the position to improve your sound system and acoustics, having the right mixer will allow you to make the best of what you already have. A mixer with superior ability to listen will maximize your investment at every level.

The challenge for most churches is that they do not have professional mixers they can rely on. Most church mixers lack skills and knowledge from the professional world. Since the price of gear cannot hide untrained ears behind the sound board, it is no surprise that many churches still suffer from mediocre sonics after spending thousands of dollars on equipment.

The amount of money invested in equipment should always reflect the amount of training invested in men. There is really no way around it. Reversing the priorities by purchasing equipment without also nurturing the skill level of your sound team will only lead to unnecessary spending.

Training vs. Hiring

Yes, training is a must! It is absolutely essential to provide proper training for your team in order for them to excel in operating sound at your church. Firstly, your sound team needs to be professionally informed (trained by professionals). Secondly, they need to be trained specifically to become experts on the needs of your church. If you are currently unsure about who should be operating sound at your church, training will allow you to first assess your people and then recruit the most capable and willing persons to be a part of your sound team.

Another option, of course, is to hire professionals for your church to take advantage of the equipment you already have. Personally, I think that this only works as a good temporary solution and should not substitute for training your own team. For instance, having a substitute preacher is fine for a few weeks, but to maintain a high standard of accountability, each church must have their very own preaching pastor.

Similarly, hiring a professional from outside the church is a good temporary solution, but to truly have mixers who will care about the needs of your church and be held accountable for their work, it is better to train and hire someone from within your own congregation.

Consider this. Hiring from outside the church gives you two options, a non-believer or a believer. Of course there is nothing wrong with hiring a non-believer to mix your weekly service, just as there is nothing wrong with hiring non-believers to renovate your church building. Though unlike a contractor, a mixer is someone with whom you and your church members will interact on a weekly basis.

A non-believer would never be able to engage the same way a believer would. He could not be held accountable to the highest standard, and he would not have a natural understanding of the needs of the church. He would not be able to participate effectively as your partner in ministry.

A believer on the other hand who attends a different church would have a better understanding of the church, but you would be taking him away from his primary fellowship. Do not underestimate the importance of being able to hold your own team accountable. Hiring operators from outside your church should preferably be considered only as a temporary solution.

Service Cannot Replace Worship

A common struggle that many behind-the-scenes volunteers share is a false sense of self-importance. Speaking from first hand knowledge, we feel in control. We associate ourselves with the people on stage, deeming ourselves above those around us. We feel in charge of the service and focus the spotlight, at least in our own minds, on ourselves. It is far too easy for sound teams to lose perspective and focus on the wrong things when they are so busy serving others weekly.

For years I mixed for my church's college ministry regularly. I was excited to be able to serve my church with my expertise every week. I showed up early and stayed late. I was happy to be involved. Little did I know that I was slowly slipping away. I saw my friends from church every week, but I was not really engaged in fellowship and worship. I eventually hit a wall. I was exhausted. Attending church became a chore.

It dawned on me that I had replaced worship with service. I was not truly concerned for my church. Even though I stayed busy serving, I had forgotten my first love in Jesus

Christ. I missed being able to worship without distractions.

Attending church every week without engaging in true worship builds a spiritual callus. Make sure that your team is not only serving the church but also being served as a part of your church. They cannot replace worship with service. They too need to be active participants of corporate worship and fellowship. Guiding your team's focus back towards worship will not only promote accountability, it will ultimately produce good stewardship, which will guide your spending and investment decisions soundly, even through extreme subjectivity.

Different Standards of Good

Having a team of skilled sound operators will provide your church with consistency in quality from week to week, and having a team full of servants and worshippers will establish a standard that is devoted to the needs of your church. However, this does not change that sound is always going to be subjective. You will need to navigate through extreme subjectivity in order to guide your church through making important investment decisions.

In the same way that you would seek to discern someone's heart when they disagree with a sermon, you need to get to the root of various concerns and complaints regarding sound. You must also make the right decisions to ensure the quality of sound. What makes a great system for one church may not be suitable for yours. How do you go about establishing a standard that is excellent and suitable for your church? How far do you need to invest in your sound system to establish a standard?

A simple indicator is your congregation's response during worship. Of course whether people are passionately worshipping is dependent upon many factors, but it can also be very telling about whether their hearts are being served or whether they are distracted by the sound.

Your congregation will sing well if they feel comfortable. If it is too loud, it will become painful and distracting. If it is too soft, it lacks impact. It discourages them from participating. Their comfort level is an indicator of the sonic quality. A well-balanced, musical mix removes distraction and points worshippers towards Christ. When the mix is really serving the congregation, they may not be able to verbalize it, but they will respond by singing with more enthusiasm.

We Stand Divided

We live in an age when everyone seems to be an expert. A quick browse on Yelp dot com, a popular restaurant review site, will reveal that everyone has contradicting tastes and opinions. Like musical preferences, these opinions can also be very deceiving. Almost every restaurant with the highest ratings is also accompanied by bad reviews.

Preferences reveal inconsistencies and can jade one's opinions and feelings. Reading a review of an Indian restaurant written by someone who hates Indian food is hardly fair. When there is bitterness towards certain styles of music, the comfort level of your congregation will cease to be an accurate indicator of sonics. Complaints about sound in churches are often not at all about sound, they are simply an expression of likes and dislikes toward certain styles of music.

We are all familiar with the division over music styles in churches today, and it is a real problem that should not be taken lightly. For some churches, it is revealed through attitudes in the congregation, for others it is revealed through church splits. Some churches design their music program based on public vote, and some people even choose their church based upon the style of music used in the worship service. Members and sometimes worship pastors leave their churches over a difference of opinions on music styles. People are opinionated when it comes to sound within a church, but they are often driven by discontentment and personal preferences. No church should be bound by one particular style of music, but many are bound by the congregation's personal preference of music. Musical styles affect how a sound operator mixes and in some cases how a sound system is setup.

We should not stand divided. If this is indeed a hurdle that your church must overcome, investing in a better sound system will not solve your problems. It is necessary to focus your congregation back onto the right things and not to let sound or music become a stumbling block to their worship.

Unity Trumps All

Worship is the appropriate response when confronted by our awesome God, and unity is a direct result of that genuine worship. Unity is the foundation of all church bodies. It even affects how sound is delivered to the congregation. If your church is splitting over the type of music used in worship, a well-trained sound team will not remedy that, neither will endless investment in better equipment. The quality of mixing becomes irrelevant.

It might be true that some genres of music are more worshipful than others. They appeal to broader audiences and allow for people to focus on the words being sung. Other styles of music, on the contrary, appeal to smaller niches. Nobody can decide that for you. It is up to you to discern what is best for your congregation. Unity is a much needed ingredient to nurture your church to maturity. It is also a much needed ingredient for your sound ministry to reach its fullest potential.

Where there is division, there is always an unhealthy amount of attention directed towards it. Help your church focus on the right things.

Think Far, Think Big

Spend for the Future

There should always be a healthy desire for God to add to your congregation through proclamation of gospel truth. Properly budgeting for each phase of growth extends beyond building a great sound system for your church. It reflects your desire for the lost to be saved. Do not limit your thinking with regards to what God will do to draw more people to Himself by failing to budget accordingly for the future.

Many churches after spending thousands of dollars ultimately end up with the wrong sound system because future plans were not taken into account. Spending for each phase must be guided by a clear vision for the future. Thinking far and thinking big is a must.

Determining a budget is no easy task. You are trained and equipped to make ministry related decisions, but you are probably not prepared to make equipment related decisions. The right operators or consultants can assist you in identifying and addressing the real needs in your church and guide you in the right direction. What they cannot do is take the lead in establishing a vision that connects all facets of your church's spending.

Sound systems are often costly and can easily become exorbitantly expensive if budgets for different phases of expansion are not carefully planned. Just like any other budgeting discipline, spending should not be focused only on the present. Inventory should be skillfully and purposefully put together. A budget incorporating long term goals for your sound system must be established in order to prevent overspending.

Big corporations base their vision of spending on expansion of profit. Every dollar they spend is viewed as an investment aimed at a higher return. A salary for the right employee is aimed towards better productivity. Leasing an office at a better location provides them with a better image amongst their competition.

Churches may share many of the same accounting principles, but their vision should be founded on ministry and stewardship. Churches do not answer to shareholders. They answer to God. Responsible and purposeful budgeting is the best way for churches to demonstrate godly stewardship.

Should we buy more land to expand the church building? Should we hire another pastor to meet increasing needs of a growing church? Should we upgrade our sound system to accommodate a larger congregation? Why are we spending money on our sound system when we could use those funds to support our missionaries in the field?

Is it sufficient to say it just sounds better? You need not understand the specifics of every purchase, but you should be prepared to give a good and supported response. Answering these questions will help to keep you accountable on spending.

Of course most church members will not inquire about every piece of equipment you purchase, but they should be able to trust that God's money is being spent strategically on real needs and that you are setting the ultimate example as God's steward. If your church budgets properly, giving an account to your congregation about your spending on sound equipment should be straightforward.

Building Legos with Sound

Many churches begin by purchasing the cheapest equipment they can find with very little thought or concern for the future. They fail to take into consideration how church growth may affect what they might need in the future or which equipment they could keep and expand upon. When the time comes for them to grow and invest in the next system, they would have no choice but to get rid of most equipment and repurchase from scratch. In terms of sound stewardship, there is nothing more wasteful. You should always purchase with the possibility of growth in mind. A common mistake is to view different phases of expansion as disjointed, unrelated pieces. Over time this becomes unnecessarily and exponentially expensive as the same mistake repeats through each phase.

Imagine teaching your son how to build a house with Legos. You have a limited budget, so you buy a cheap Lego copy set from Fake Lego Inc with ten Lego pieces for the base of the house. A month goes by, and you get a raise in salary, which affords you to buy the genuine Lego set from Real Lego Inc. Because these Legos came from two different manufacturers, the pieces are not compatible with each other. The base you built cannot be added upon with the new Lego house set. With no other choice, you are forced to purchase an extra base from Real Lego Inc to finish building the house, which further adds to your cost.

Too often, churches fall into the same trap of buying the fake Lego set, because it is initially cheaper, only to find themselves spending more money than intended later. If you expect that you will need a digital console down the road, do not settle for a mediocre version now simply because you cannot afford the real thing. Also, if you know that you will need more sound for your next space, do not buy standalone speakers that cannot be added upon.

Be patient, and maximize what you already have until the right moment to buy. Different phases of growth should be viewed as different pieces of the same puzzle. It is crucial to connect the different phases, maximizing on previous investments.

Just as a bad tree cannot bear good fruit, quality sound cannot come from a bad sounding room. Acoustics function as the base on which the puzzle rests. If investing in equipment and skilled operators represent the seeds which you are sowing, then the quality of the acoustics represents the soil that determines whether the seeds will grow.

You already know the importance of focusing on the foundation. Sound investments should first be prioritized with acoustical treatment and lastly with equipment purchase. The acoustics of your worship space is the foundation of good sonic quality.

Many churches overspend because their worship space lacks the infrastructure for good acoustics. Churches fix their problems by purchasing more equipment instead of investing in critical acoustical treatments. Good acoustics allow you to hear your investment through quality equipment. When budgeting for sound, infrastructure should take first priority whenever your situation allows. Investing in acoustics is no doubt a serious financial commitment, but it will be a worthy and lasting investment that saves precious funds in the long run.

Three Phases of Growth

Approximately sixty percent of churches have a
congregation of fewer than two hundred members. Many
churches either do not own a building or simply cannot
afford to renovate the existing infrastructure. Less than two
percent of churches in the United States are mega churches
with over six thousand people. You are more likely to be
pastoring a small to medium sized church rather than a
mega church with thousands of members. Still, you should
always aim and expect your church to grow.

Most churches go through three phases of growth in relation
to sound with each phase benchmarking the growth of a
church. These phases of growth apply to most churches
regardless of their size. Understanding these phases of
growth will help you be a good steward of your church's
funds by making the right choices with sound investments.
Structuring your budget accordingly and creatively will help
you prepare for future expansion.

A creative budget can be established with an even approach
through various stages. Instead of planning for a small initial
investment and exponentially increasing the budget in later

phases, churches should consider making a medium sized investment spread out over the course of a few phases and focusing on purchasing equipment that works as a foundation that can be expanded upon. You can establish a vision that stretches beyond your current stage of growth by creatively rethinking how each phase of audio expansion can be budgeted. Smaller churches generally need less equipment, which in turn imposes a smaller financial burden. They can afford to extend their budget and make quality purchases that would benefit them beyond the present.

When running a marathon, the world's best athletes maintain fairly even speeds throughout their races. They may fluctuate slightly as they employ different tactics depending on the terrain and their own physique, but you do not see them creating a very steep climb for themselves by jogging slowly in the beginning and sprinting full speed at the end.

Church administrators should take a similar approach by making good initial investments and buying quality gear. Imagine yourself running a marathon. I realize that you might have a smaller budget if your church is small, but even still, you should not be deterred from strategically purchasing the right gear that would benefit later phases of expansion.

It is much easier to grow into your needs than to need something you do not own. A general rule of thumb when purchasing equipment is to 'buy up'. Buying up simply means purchasing quality gear that exceeds your current needs. This principle should apply regardless of whether you are purchasing a personal computer or a mixing console for your church. Purchasing an old computer right before the new version is released would only cost you more money and frustration. Your old computer will not support the latest software, and very soon, you are in the market for another computer when you could have purchased the new computer in the first place. Within the confines of your budget, purchase a couple things that would carry you through to the next phase. Discuss with your team what those key purchases could be.

Phase One: Thinking Far and Thinking Big

As a smaller church, you are not likely to have expenses like child-care facilities and bathroom upgrades, which could afford you to allocate a healthy budget for the initial phase, depending on what resources are available to you. If you are already planning to expand your existing building or construct another worship space in the near future, saving for later phases will be a good idea. The key is in maintaining balance with current needs while planning for the future.

Thinking far and thinking big by purchasing quality gear now that can later be easily added to is a responsible use of funds. Certain speakers, for example, are designed to be stackable, making expansion a much easier transition. You can also save funds by finding a worship space with workable acoustics. Having the right acoustics will eliminate many costs. It is also a more rewarding space in which to operate sound.

If you do not have access to a good acoustic space, there are a number of acoustical treatments you can consider without having to do major construction to your building. Carpeting instead of hard floors, installing bass traps in the corners and hanging ceiling treatments are all more affordable potential alternatives to renovation. It will be helpful to bring along an acoustician to help you assess a location. And doing so will even help you establish strong relationships early on with sound professionals who can become increasingly helpful allies in training men and planning for later phases.

When starting out with a smaller congregation, you also have to decide what is the best use of your limited manpower. The type of equipment you choose can either lengthen or shorten your setup and tear-down time.

When I attended college, I led worship for a fellowship group of about sixty people every week. We built a system with two speakers, a twenty-four channel mixing console and a one hundred foot snake. It took three hours every week to load, unload, setup, sound check and tear down. We were committed to it because it worked with our vision, and we had enough young, enthusiastic students to help. But it is essential for you to decide what is the best use of resources for your church.

Portable systems with separate mixing boards and speaker amplifiers are good examples of a system that can be added upon and will allow room for growth, but it will also require more setup time. If your church is very limited in human resources, purchasing a system with a built in mixer would be the smarter choice. Musicians could set themselves up and be self-sufficient.

Phase Two: At The Crossroads

As a church grows in size, their expenses grow along with them. In this phase, you are probably upgrading to a large-scale system for the first time, and it can seem like a sudden jump in cost.

Many churches in fear of over-spending will choose the lowest cost options in this phase to fulfill their immediate needs. Instead of purchasing with a clear vision for the future, churches often purchase equipment with low expansion compatibility that they will prematurely outgrow. I can assure you that it is less burdensome to make a few big purchases now than to be forced to purchase everything, a console, eight line array speakers and eight new power amplifiers, and still have to do construction on your new building all at the same time.

In this phase, you are at the most pivotal point of equipment purchase. The size of these purchases is large enough to impact future spending and budgets. Statistics say that most churches will not outgrow a building that fits one thousand people. It is at this stage that churches are standing at a crossroads.

A church either continues to expand, outgrowing their current building, or they divide into smaller churches to reach out to farther communities. Their decisions greatly impact both current and future sound needs. What they purchase now will determine what they need to purchase in the next phase. I have consulted for many churches in this phase that were stuck with a system that was seemingly sufficient at the time of purchase but outgrew it before they were financially ready for the next expansion and upgrade.

Conversely, if your church decides not to expand into a larger worship space, your investment should not be focused on the ability to deliver high volumes to reach a larger crowd. Instead you should focus your investments on quality upgrades. Purchase quality microphones, cables and better quality musical instruments that will all contribute to the integrity of sound. Purchase the console you know you will need even if your worship band is not complex enough to utilize it to the fullest. On the other hand, if your church is planning on moving to a larger building, then your investment efforts should be focused on the ability to deliver enough sound to a large crowd.

Not long ago, I visited a church in Hollywood, California that was meeting in a high school auditorium. They did not have a permanent building, so they were setting up from scratch every week. I noticed that they had a very large stack of high-end speakers. The volume was not overbearing, and it was operated skillfully.

This church was planning on moving into a bigger building, and they knew that they would outgrow their building soon. So they bought (up) and invested in more sound power than they currently need. Just because you have equipment that is capable of delivering a lot of volume does not mean that you have to drive it to its fullest capacity. This church focused their investment efforts in the right direction by purchasing equipment capable of delivering enough sound for a larger space.

Being at the crossroads does not mean that you have to sacrifice sound quality for volume, or vice versa. Quality gear does not deliver less volume. Focusing on the right features to invest in will allow you to maximize your funds. Understanding the needs and plans specific to your church will help you and your team purchase equipment with the correct technical specifications.

Phase Three: Reaching Beyond Thousands

Most church buildings do not hold over three thousand people, in fact, less than two percent of all churches in the United States exceed this size. A space of this size is not usually readily available. Unless built to specifications, you will most likely be constructing a church building or campus from the ground up.

At this stage, you are likely not only to need a system that can deliver enough sound to thousands of people in the worship space, you would also need your sound to network and support other facets of your ministry. Many churches of this size have a television broadcast, radio networks, and recording booths as well as seminaries and bible colleges. Your sound needs far exceed the parameter of the sanctuary. You are putting together a system that can reach beyond thousands of people.

A system of this size will undoubtedly be extremely expensive, and any mistakes made will most likely be exponentially more expensive. Renovating a large church means displacing thousands of people. The system you install in this phase will likely remain in place for quite some time. For this reason, it is essential that you place paramount emphasis on the foundations of sound. Set your priorities right, beginning with proper acoustical treatment.

It is easy to feel overwhelmed by expenses. Many churches at this stage risk losing sight of their vision and foregoing many important aspects of sound system design. I urge you to learn from their mistakes and avoid overspending for years to come.

Before drafting any plans, consult with an acoustician as well as a sound system designer. Then invite your designers and contractors to your regular services to help them understand the requirements of your worship service. Explain your vision to them. A clear vision will keep the acoustician and sound-system designer on target.

Hire the right people and stick with your vision.

The Ultimate Focus

It is not my intention for this book to make sound the focus of your church, but it is most definitely my intention to remove all distractions that could be caused by sound. I want you to adjust your thinking when making investment decisions on sound so that you and your church will not waver from the ultimate focus: worshipping our Savior.

Pursuing excellence is not an option. It is a command. Consider these words as you challenge yourself in thinking through the pursuit of excellence:

"God's standards are perfection, and they've been met in Jesus Christ who lived a perfect life in our place and died as our substitute, enduring the wrath of God in our place. ALL our offerings, no matter how well or poorly offered, are perfected through the once and for all offering of the Savior. We can strive for excellence to serve others, while extending to others the same grace we've received." - Bob Kauflin

We should be united in reinforcing the gospel message behind everything we do, so that no one can mistake our efforts for anything other than our love for Christ and each other. I pray that you will see and hear the fruits of your hard work and that sound transforms from what was once a frustrating mystery into something that has become your true partner in ministry, proclaiming truth with great strength and, most importantly, with clarity.

The Bottom Line: Be Creative

Planning, budgeting and building a sound system is no easy task, but you did not waive all challenges when God chose you to lead His church. It is your responsibility to provide guidance, instruction and encouragement for your church. Churches of different sizes each have their own needs, but they share many of the same struggles. They all share the fundamental problem of reversed priorities in their thinking about investment in sound.

The appropriate sound system for your church is not always an expensive system. You have to decide what is the best system to suit the needs of your church given the specific resources available to you. Take into consideration the size, styles of music, level of musicianship and technical skills of your sound team.

You have probably already realized that reading this book does not make you a sound guy. You are, however, a visionary qualified to lead your sound team, musicians and contractors in establishing a sound vision for your church. Your vision for your sound ministry should reflect a desire to be a good steward. You need to make use of all resources available to you and to your church.

For sound to have a positive impact on your church (yet remain invisible and free of distractions) takes a lot of planning and creativity. Work with your team and challenge them. Share this book with them and discuss how best to apply these principles specifically for your church. Choose the right people. And with sufficient training, they will be more than qualified to help you address the true needs of your church.

I did not give you a step-by-step guide to investing in sound. Instead I gave you the necessary resources and principles to apply in order to establish your own sound vision for your church. The bottom line is: be creative and consult with the most knowledgeable and experienced people that understand and love the church.

Think far and think big, and you will hear the fruits of your labor. This is a great opportunity to grow with your church body and explore the real meaning of worship. Help them focus on the right things.

AUDIO MUST PREACH

Debtcibel is not intended to provide a solution to every audio situation but to help establish right thinking about sound ministry at your church. We would love to hear from you to know how this book has helped you or if you have any questions or concerns.

Write to us at contact@audiomustpreach.com. We promise you a personal response. You can also visit our website at audiomustpreach.com.

Acknowledgements

I would like to express my love and deep appreciation for my wife, Audra. She has made this book a possibility not only through her unwavering support and encouragement but also through her hard work as chief editor of *debtcibel* and director of Audio Must Preach. She is also the best mother to our son, Lucien.

Also, many thanks to the following people who have played an influential role in inspiring me to write this book:

Robert Fong, Evelyn Fong, Daniel Fong, Charis Fong, John Martin, Rick Holland, John MacArthur, Jonathan Rourke, Malcolm du Plessis, Bob Kauflin, Joshua Spacht, Andy Snider, Bill Schnee, Russ Castillo, Ritchie Huang, Grace Huang, Seth Godin, Jason Friedman

About the Author

Darius Fong is a Grammy winning sound engineer whose real passion is the 'Church'. He is the founder of **Audio Must Preach**, an independent resource dedicated to helping churches remove audio related obstacles, with a focus on ministry and stewardship. He has consulted for churches around the world as well as conferences such as the Resolved Conference and the Shepherd's Conference.

A Hong Kong native, Darius began his career in music and audio, at the age of 18, building and designing speaker systems for large stadiums and arenas. Darius received his Bachelor of Arts degree in Telecommunications from Indiana University. Darius currently resides in Los Angeles with his wife, Audra, and his two year old son, Lucien.